The Mindset of Small Talk

How mastering small talk has nothing to do with coming up with things to say

BY:

Lana Otoya

© **Copyright 2018 - All rights reserved.**

The contents of this book may not be reproduced, duplicated or transmitted without direct written permission from the author.

Under no circumstances will any legal responsibility or blame be held against the publisher for any reparation, damages, or monetary loss due to the information herein, either directly or indirectly.

Legal Notice:

This book is copyright protected. This is only for personal use. You cannot amend, distribute, sell, use, quote or paraphrase any part or the content of this book without the consent of the author.

Disclaimer Notice:

Please note the information contained in this document is for educational and entertainment purposes only. Every attempt has been made to provide accurate, up to date and reliable, complete information. No warranties of any kind are expressed or implied. Readers acknowledge that the author is not engaging in the rendering of legal, financial, medical or professional advice. The content of this book has been derived from various sources. Please consult a licensed professional before attempting any techniques outlined in this book.

By reading this document, the reader agrees that under no circumstances is the author responsible for any losses, direct or indirect, which are incurred as a result of the use of information contained within this document, including, but not limited to, — errors, omissions, or inaccuracies.

Table of Contents

INTRODUCTION...6

PREFACE: SMALL TALK IS A SKILL............10

Chapter One: A Shift in Perspective..............13

Chapter Two: Don't Talk..............................20

Chapter Three: Show Genuine Interest........24

Chapter Four: Now for the talking bit..........33

Chapter Five: Small Talk for People with Social Anxiety..42

Chapter Six: Small Talk for introverts.........49

Chapter Seven: Small Talk for Dates............56

Chapter Eight: Small Talk for Making Friends....62

Chapter Nine: Small Talk for Networking and Business events...65

Conclusion...70

Free Bonus: 100 Conversation Starters...............72

INTRODUCTION

Hey Friend! Thanks for grabbing a copy of my book.

Small talk is an odd thing to write a book about. Especially coming from me, a deeply introverted person who hated even the thought of striking up a conversation with someone I didn't know.

When I say deeply introverted, I mean it. When I was in University, I ate lunch alone in the library because I didn't want to small talk around a group of people I didn't know. It was easier for me to bury my head in a book and wait until the lunch hour was over than strike up a meaningless conversation.

It had little to do with insecurity or even shyness. I just genuinely preferred spending my time alone rather than mingling with the other people in my film class. Little did I know back then, this was me choosing not to develop a skill that has become so valuable in my current life and something that I have used to get almost everything I've ever wanted.

Life is all about learning. Learning to develop the skills that you were not naturally born with and turning them into tools that allow you to improve your life and reach your goals.

Before we get into the nitty gritty, let me give you a brief introduction as to who I am and what my mission is.

My name is Lana and I am a relationship and self care blogger. I founded a blog called Millennialships.com which helps people strengthen themselves and their relationships in order to live a happier life.

Everything I coach about, speak about and write about – yes including this book - is based on the Millennialships concept. Millennialships stands for Millennial + Relationships. The concept is simple and is as follows:

Better Yourself

Better Your Relationships

Live a Happier Life.

When I say better yourself, I am talking about taking care of your mental health and also learning skills that will help you thrive in relationships. These skills include, healthy communication skills, how to fight in a healthy way and yes, even small talk.

The reason I focus so much on relationships is because...relationships are the key to a happy life.

Think about it.

Whenever you feel down or like you're going through the hardest time in your life, you'll often say "I don't want to talk about it" or "you won't understand." This is because you feel alone. You feel like no one will understand where you're coming from, so you rather not mention it. This is what makes people start questioning the point of life. My mission in life – and what the Millennialships concept is all about - is to remind everyone that the point of life is *people*.

So what does this have to do with small talk? Small talk is a chore. It's not something we easily want to do or take part in yet...

Small talk was the first conversation you had with your best friend. It was the first conversation you had with your boss. It was the first conversation you had (or will have) with the love of your life. All meaningful relationships that are not family relationships started with a conversation that was simple, mundane and didn't have a deeper meaning. Therefore learning and adopting this skill will do wonders for your life. It is the first step to love, financial security (think job interviews) and eventually, happiness.

In summary, small talk leads to relationships and relationships lead to happiness. Once you understand this mindset, *the mindset of small talk,* you can start to see that there is so much more to this skill than memorizing a bunch of conversation starters. It's about changing your perspective and realizing how much small talk actually does for *you.*

So please, take all this advice to heart but don't beat yourself up if it doesn't come naturally right away. It is a skill, like riding a bike. Some people never learn how to ride a bike and others can jump their bike forty feet in the air and spin it around before landing safely on the ground. I say if we land somewhere in the middle of that, we'll be in an excellent place.

PREFACE: SMALL TALK IS A SKILL

Have you ever found yourself in a "the weather is nice isn't it?" conversation with someone? Did the struggle seem worse than an engineering exam? If that doesn't scare you, imagine being at a party – you are having a conversation with someone and you suddenly run out of things to talk about. Jumping out of the window may seem like your best escape route, but it isn't the most sustainable option. So how is it that some people are able to chat non-stop, yet you're there contemplating how badly the jump out the window is going to hurt.

The truth is, everyone hates small talk to some level, but some people are able to use it to their advantage and make the best out of it. Mastering small talk can provide us with the social lubricant we need in order to stay connected to people. You may not believe it right now but, with some effort, you will get a little better at it, then a lot better at it, then master it. It takes practice, but you will get there and I'm here to help.

As you know, I hated small talk but eventually realized that small talk is exactly what you need to bridge the gap between two people. Contrary to the popular belief that small talk only refers to small and superfluous conversations, it is the stepping-stone you need to build meaningful relationships. Once I accepted this, it was a lot easier to engage in mundane conversations because I was no longer above it all. So If you wish to strike up a conversation with that interesting stranger, you have to get past the existential dread associated with it. It's less about thinking of a laundry list of conversation starters and more about changing your mindset. This mindset shift will make small talk easier and then practicing it will make it even easier than that. Again, this is a skill that must be practiced, it has nothing to do with natural ability or even being introverted or extroverted.

When I was younger I hated parties. I would spend an abnormal amount of time nervously hiding around the corner because I was bad at small talk. However back then, I didn't consider myself "bad at small talk." I just told myself I didn't like parties. It was this kind of mentality that stopped me from trying to improve my small talk skills. I didn't tell myself I was "bad at it," instead I just told myself I "wasn't interested." That mindset allowed me to justify not learning a new skill and not going out of my comfort zone. By telling myself I wasn't interested or that "I only enjoy deep and meaningful conversations," I was hurting myself. I was stopping myself from meeting new people and making new friends.

This book contains everything you thought was dreadful about small talk. Whether you have social anxiety, you're an introvert like me, you wish to network, want to make more friends or you are looking for the love of your life, I have something for everyone in this book. The first step is knowing that small talk is a skill and if you weren't born with it, don't fret because few people are.

Chapter One: A Shift in Perspective

The reason you're "bad" at small talk or "don't like it" is because you're not looking at it through the right lens. I mentioned that in University I used to sit alone at lunch time rather than small talking and making friends. I knew at the time that it might be considered a little "weird" but I wasn't insecure about this.

I didn't tell myself I was bad at making friends because I didn't think it had anything to do with that. I just was just more interested in reading books at the library, what's wrong with that? I wasn't saying to myself "aw man I wish I could go out there and chat with those cool people". Quite the opposite actually, I was saying stuff like "all they talk about is drugs and drinking and I rather read books about more intellectual things".

What I was really doing was *justifying* why I shouldn't have to make the effort.

No more justifications and excuses

Even though I might have enjoyed reading books more than talking to my classmates, my excuses and justifications were only hurting myself. There are plenty of hours in the day to read books, watch TV, play video games etc. There are much more limited hours in the day when we get exposed to potential new relationships.

It is in your best interest to jump on the opportunity to form a new relationship every time you are presented with one.

Remember that I think relationships are the key to happiness in life. So every time you turn down an opportunity to form a new relationship, you are turning down potential happiness. No good.

One of the most common complaints I hear from introverts is "I hate small talk, I much rather have a deep and meaningful conversation". Notice how I called this a "complaint" rather than a "statement". It's because that's exactly what this is, it's whining and complaining that you can't have a conversation that is more fun before you even know the person. You can't put the cart before the horse, you can't ask someone to marry you on the first date, and you can't ask someone their deepest darkest secrets during your first conversation. I didn't make the rules, I just follow them.

Human relationships take time to develop. Once you accept that a deep conversation doesn't happen without small talk happening first, you have the necessary *perspective shift* to start small talking effectively.

A skill for your life tool box

When you develop a skill that you were not naturally born with, you create a tool that you can use to improve your life. Learning a new skill is *always* a good thing. The difficulty here is the frustration that comes with not being good at something. It just doesn't feel good to be bad at something. If you're bad at small talk, it can be awkward, embarrassing and make you feel small. Not fun feelings.

The key to get around this is to tell yourself that you are good at *learning*. When you tell yourself that you are good at learning, your mind all of sudden starts to feel ok with being bad at a skill. "I might not be good at things right away, but I'm good at learning." Repeat that phrase in your head and write it down in your notebook so that you never forget it.

Let's go back to the bike example that I used in the introduction. If you're learning to ride a bike and you expect to be good at it right away, every time you fall it's going to be frustrating. Every time you fall is going to feel like a disappointment. If you tell yourself you're just learning, and you're good at learning, your perspective shifts. Now you're focusing on every milestone and accomplishment rather than every failure. If this time you rode your bike for ten feet instead of four feet, you can say to yourself "see I'm good at learning, I just taught myself how to go six feet farther."

This same principal can be applied to small talk. Every time you say something weird or the conversation gets awkward, just remind yourself that you're learning – and you're good at learning.

Don't beat yourself up

There's no social scenario worth beating yourself up about. No matter what happens, don't dwell on things that you said. What's done is done. Dwelling will only damage your confidence, and you will be less likely to continue working on your small talk skills in the future. There is no particular strategy that is designed to give guaranteed results, it's all trial and error and something that gets easier over time. Just like any skill, it needs to be practiced.

There are so many people out there wanting to make new friends that it really doesn't matter if you fail to make conversations with a few. When you find yourself inevitably dwelling on the conversation that just took place, focus your thoughts on the "takeaway lesson" for next time. And then just let it go, without any regrets. There's always a next time, and you will always do better with each conversation.

One thing that can help with not beating yourself up, or overthinking is to stop taking yourself so seriously. Funny or even awkward stories are human and relatable. Not having a perfect flow or knowing all the right words just makes you a regular old human being. In fact, being perfectly smooth and charismatic can often come across as intimidating to another person. Stories that are not perfect will lead the conversation into a comfortable zone. Humor has a way making people feel comfortable with each other, and you can use this to your advantage.

No more fearing the silent killer

Stop thinking that awkward silences mean the conversation is going badly. This is just not true! Very rarely, we bump into someone for the first time and get along like a house-on-fire. No awkward silences, no formalities, just a fun conversation that flows smoothly. But this doesn't happen too often and, in general, people are cautious about opening up with someone they don't know. It's normal to have a few nervous pauses, awkward silences and blank stares, even if you're getting along great with the person. I know it seems like a worst nightmare, but it's inevitable when you are striking up a conversation with people for the first time. So, rather than trying to avoid it, be okay with it, it doesn't always imply disinterest.

An awkward silence doesn't mean that you're failing at the conversation. The person you are chatting with could be shy or have social anxiety. They could even be tired, distracted or could be in a laid-back mood. Whatever the reason for the pause, you will make it worse if you try too hard to ward off the lulls and keep chatting mindlessly about anything that comes to your mind. If you try to fill the empty space too quickly and inauthentically, the person will sense your "fear" and they will start to feel uncomfortable.

It's even worse if you make it obvious by saying things like "soooo....." and looking awkward without coming up with something to say. The reason this is detrimental to a good conversation is because you have now done three things:

1. You've told the person that you feel awkward

2. This makes them feel awkward about the situation as well
3. You've put them on the spot because now they feel pressure to come up with something to say to save this sea of awkwardness

None of those situations are making you a fun and approachable person that people will enjoy talking to. Instead of the silence being something that you both move on from, you are putting a spotlight on it and making the other person feel like they want to get out of this, fast.

Don't fill silences with nonsocial banter, just relax. Be patient if either one of you goes completely blank in the midst of a conversation, not knowing what to say next. Allow the silence to be there for a few moments, and think of it as a transition to a better conversation.

Chapter Two: Don't Talk

It sounds backwards but one of the ways I developed my small talk skills was to stop talking so much. If you're not naturally witty or a "talker", you might feel awkward coming up with stories to tell. The good news is you don't have to do all the talking, or even half the talking. You can just encourage the other person to talk to you.

"Talk to somebody about themselves and they'll listen for hours." Good ol' Dale Carnegie came up with that quote decades ago and it will be true forever. Most people like talking about themselves, it's their favourite subject. All you have to do to be a good "talker" or be seen as a "really nice person" is to be a good listener.

Don't think, listen

Being a good listener means that you actually hear what the person was saying. You're not thinking "oh god I want to get out of here". Or "man this party sucks, I totally should have bailed".

Reduce the inner thoughts by listening. The person in front of you has all your attention. Your thoughts are the reason you are bad at small talk. Your thoughts are judging you, they are overthinking everything and they are filtering your words – it's a lot easier to be a charming talker when the voice in your head stops judging you.

Don't ramble on about yourself

Have you ever been in a conversation with somebody that just wouldn't stop talking about themselves? It gets really tiring, even if that person is your best friend. If you are going on and on about yourself, the other person is destined to get tired. That's why I made this whole chapter on "don't talk", if you are listening 75% of the time and talking the other 25% that's a really good ratio to hold the other person's interest.

All this being said, the person you are talking to will be a lot more forgiving if you are talking about a *topic* rather than yourself. So if you are talking a lot about how to mountain bike, the person is at least learning something new and they will be able to tolerate this for a lot longer than stories about your life.

A good conversation is like a game of ping pong, it should go back and forth. Unlike ping pong though, the best small talkers know when to let the other person take the lead and just step back and listen.

Body language is your best friend

Using the appropriate body language is *even more* important than coming up with the "right" things to say. Body language communicates things to other people that would be very difficult to communicate with words.

For example, you can use body language to show someone that you're listening. Since you can't say "yes I am listening and hearing you", you have to "say" those things with your body. You nod and make facial expressions that respond the story. If they are telling you about the time they broke their leg, you cringe or open your eyes wide to show that the story is having an impact on you.

This will show them you're engaged in the conversation and it will encourage them to keep talking. You absolutely cannot be engaged in a conversation if your mind is occupied with other things and using your body to react to the story is a great way to stay present. It's a way to keep you focused on the conversation and take away the negative Nancy inside your head.

Body language is also the easiest "conversation starter". Make sure your body language is telling people that you'd love to start a conversation. If you come across as closed off and reserved, people will not be interested in striking up any conversation with you. This includes looking at your phone which is the number one way to turn people off from approaching you in a social situation. This body language is telling them you are not interested in talking, not a very good way to small talk!

Using body language as a conversation starter means that you don't have to think of a silly question or comment to insert yourself into a conversation. You simply use your body.

An example of when to use this is when you want to insert yourself into a group of people who are already talking. You can do this by smiling or laughing at a comment that was just made or simply giving a small wave while you position yourself inside this circle. You do this so that you don't have to interrupt the person that is talking but your body language is saying "I would like to be part of the conversation". Of course you would never want to actually say that statement out loud. Using body language to gain approval from the group is a much more natural transition.

Chapter Three: Show Genuine Interest

Having a genuine interest in the people you are talking to, no matter who they are is SO IMPORTANT when it comes to small talk. This is the one step that will take you from an okay small talker to an AMAZING one. People might even refer to you as a real "people person" if you nail this one down.

One of the nicest ladies I ever met was a school teacher. I was chatting with her on a film set once because we were using her daughter in a commercial. This lady was (and I repeat) one of the *nicest people I have ever met.* I think we chatted for about thirty minutes and then I never saw her again.

Thirty. Minutes.

I seriously thought that I could trust this lady with all my deepest darkest secrets. That I could call her up one day and ask her to go for coffee and she'd say yes.

How could this lady make such an impression on me in such a short amount of time?

The answer is that she was genuinely interested in *everything* I had to say. With every word that came out of my mouth, she responded with **enthusiasm** and **intrigue.** These two things are they keys to successful small talking. If you master only these two things, you will master small talking.

Enthusiasm

The actual definition of enthusiasm is the following: *intense and eager enjoyment, interest, or approval.*

See how it says intense and eager? When you're chatting with someone you don't know, the quickest and easiest way to gain their trust is to show enthusiasm. Yes, basically an exaggerated happiness to things they say. This doesn't mean that you act "fake", quite the opposite.

It means that you really want to hear their story and you're not going to judge them no matter what they say. You respond positively and excitedly to whatever they tell you because you want to hear more.

"Wow you water ski? Damn that is so cool! I'd be way too nervous to do that."

"Omg that's your puppy?? He's SOOO cute! I wish I had a puppy like that."

"You do cocaine binges every weekend? Wow! You must love to party, what kind of music do you listen to?"

What you're doing when you respond enthusiastically to what they are saying is you're subconsciously telling them two things:

1. They are entertaining you with what they are saying. This makes them feel good.

2. You approve of them.

The second point is the most important one. When humans are put into social situations where they may be uncomfortable, the biggest thing they want to be is *accepted*. In order to be accepted, the other people in the room must approve of them. What you do by responding enthusiastically to their stories is you're telling them that you approve of them.

If they tell you something personal, like "I really love playing video games on my PC" and you respond with "oh wow that's so nerdy." You are not accepting them and you are closing the connection that you might have had with this person. You have now lost their trust and they will be less likely to keep telling you things and even less likely to want to be your friend.

You want the person you are talking to trust you. This helps establish a bond that may last only for the duration of the conversation, or for the duration of your friendship with them.

I want to take this moment to be very clear about something here. Being genuine means that you are honest and transparent. So when you approve of someone or respond enthusiastically, this doesn't mean you have to agree with everything they say. The last thing you want to be in a conversation with a new person is fake. If they don't see right through you at the beginning, they will see through you if you start becoming friends. The whole point of small talk is to attempt to forge a relationship that you might take with you beyond that party, that one date or that networking event.

Approval means that you don't judge or criticize them, it doesn't mean you agree with everything. If they say something like they do cocaine binges every weekend, you respond honestly with something like: "oh wow that sounds crazy but I could never do that, I'm way too straight edge." Being honest and stating your opinion in a nice way is also a great way to start moving the conversation away from small talk and toward something more meaningful.

I know I talked about body language in the last chapter, but body language is an incredible way to show enthusiasm. Using facial expressions, even slightly exaggerated ones is a great way to encourage the other person to keep talking.

Have you ever had a conversation with someone that you knew wasn't listening to you? It sucks. You're going on and on and the person is clearly thinking of something else or looking at their phone and you just know you're not getting anywhere with this person. The feeling you're feeling in that moment is rejection. You always want to make the person who is talking to you feel accepted. The more you do this, and on an even greater level (ie. laughing at their jokes) the more highly they will think of *you* as a person.

If you are laughing at their jokes and agreeing with their frustrations the more they will think "wow that guy (or girl) was such a great person, I had so much fun talking to them."

Intrigue

The other thing that made that lady so nice and awesome to talk to was that she showed intrigue. She was curious to learn more about all the things I talked about, yes *all of them*. So if I said that I was into mountain biking, she would ask follow up questions as though she wanted to take up mountain biking herself.

Imagine that your favourite thing in the whole world is knitting. You live and breathe knitting. Then you mention to me that you like knitting and I act as though I might want to do it myself. I ask questions like:

Wow, that's so cool- what kind of things do you make?

Is it hard to learn, did it take you many years?

What's something easy to knit that a beginner could do?

These questions all show genuine interest in your favourite topic. It's going to get you talking and talking about how to knit and even if I don't care at all about knitting, you do and this conversation is making you very happy.

Follow up questions show the person that you'd like to hear more about what they're saying. You're subconsciously telling them "wow you're interesting, tell me more, I'm interested in you". That's the nicest compliment a human can give to another human.

The key here, and the thing that made that lady stand out to me so much was that she did this with *everything* I said. There was not a place that I could take the conversation where she wasn't willing to come with me. This made me feel very comfortable and safe. It made me feel like I could really start opening up and this person would hear me out, approve of me and want to know more.

You might be thinking, but what if they start talking about something I don't know anything about? Something I don't care about. Well that's even better! If you don't know anything about it, that means you have something to learn. If someone is interested in a certain topic, it must be interesting on some level. Even if they like accounting and mathematics, you could ask them something like: "most people think that stuff is boring, what do you see in it that makes it so fun?" Boom. Now you've led them to a place where they are going to tell you why it's fun and you don't have to say anything about it. They're doing all the talking!

A genuine escape

A small talk conversation can only go so far. If you are genuinely connecting with the person and having a good time, the "small talk" part of it will go away quickly and you'll just be in a real conversation.

If you find that the conversation is staying on the small talk level for too long, it's good to have a polite way to get out so as not to make things weird. At a party, the best way to do this is to "go to the bathroom" or to "get a drink," easy. Same goes for any networking event.

On a date, it's best to have first dates on a weeknight so that you can always say "well I better get going, I have work in the morning." It's a polite escape that is perfectly understandable and doesn't hurt the other person's feelings.

It's perfectly fine to end a conversation if you're not feeling it. The fact that you started the conversation and tried the person out is all you need to do to make friends and meet people. No need to prolong the suffering, just be confident in your escape route and use it when necessary.

Chapter Four: Now for the talking bit

Ok here's where we get down to the nitty gritty. We've covered mindset, body language, listening and being genuine, none of which have to do with actually talking. Now we get to the one step that really doesn't feel natural and falls the most into a "learned skill" category. This one is pure memorization and practice. Trying to remember these topics and conversation starters will be difficult when you're feeling nervous, shy and put on the spot. This is the hard part.

The good thing about having some solid conversation topics is that you can always pull from them. If the conversation gets awkward or slows down, you can pull out one of these and be sure to continue the conversation for a few more minutes.

There are literally millions of these so instead of listing off a bunch of conversation starters and general topics. I'm going to breakdown what makes a good one and what makes a bad one so that it can help you come up with your own list. Before we get into it though, I want to point out that I don't think a conversation starter is the same as a conversation topic. Conversation starters to me are phrases that you use to *start* a conversation, meaning that you have not yet started talking to the person. Conversation topics are phrases or questions you ask in order to keep the conversation going.

Bad conversation starters

If you Google "conversation starters" a lot of them are really bad and many of them aren't starters at all, they are topics that you would bring up in the middle of a conversation. I want to tell you why these are bad so that you can formulate good conversation starters and not get trapped using ones like these.

The first bad one is commenting about the weather. Yes these are bad, I have used them in desperate situations but then quickly change the subject into something more interesting. For example:

Me: "man it sure is rainy today!"

Other person: "sure is, downpouring."

Here is where the conversation could die a slow awkward death. That is why this conversation starter is really bad unless you're quick on your toes and ready to save it. I don't like putting myself in situations where I have to save something at the top of my head so I really try to avoid the weather comments. As a bonus, I'll show you how I'd save this conversation.

Other person: "sure is, downpouring."

Me: "All the more reason to head to Mexico! For some reason I always end up booking my vacations in the summer time but the rainy spring time is when I should be doing it. Don't you think?"

Now we can segway into talking about vacations. Conversation saved, but not easily.

Another bad conversation starter is a super generic one like "What's your story?" or "Tell me about yourself?" These are bad because they are way too vague and put the person completely on the spot. If you actually said these in a conversation with someone, they would definitely think you're weird. What's your story? Who says that. Don't make the conversation starter too vague or personal.

Another example of a bad one is something like "do you listen to any podcasts, what's your favorite?" Now I know I said above that you don't want to ask questions that are too vague but ones that are too specific are also bad. Not *everyone* I know listens to podcasts so the answer to this question could very well be "no, I don't listen to any." Now the conversation is dead and you have to save it with another question. This question is much better used as a conversation topic if you've been chatting with the person for a little while and just need something to keep it going. In that case, if they say they do not listen to podcasts, you could bring up a podcast that you listen to that you think they might like. This is much easier to do if you've been chatting and have already learned a few things about them.

Good conversation starters

The best conversation starters are really simple and natural. They are not fancy. They are boring and mundane and that's what makes them great. You can use them in any situation to get the conversation started. Now remember, a conversation starter is not a question that you ask mid way through a conversation so that you can keep it going. That is why starters like "what do you do to waste time?" make no sense. How are you going to walk up to someone and start a conversation like that? Most of the starters I see online are way too specific

It's really good to try and match your conversation starters up with your favourite topics so that you can expand on them. For example any comment about movies or filmmaking is a great one for me because I worked in the film industry and am passionate about filmmaking. Try to make your conversation starters match your interests. Here are some examples of actual conversation starters that you can use to start chatting with anyone.

"Hey I'm Lana, I don't think we've met."

"Hey what kind of beer (or other drink) is that? I don't think I've tried it" or, "nice, you're drinking (insert drink) that's my favourite IPA"

"Hey haven't seen you for a while, what's new? still working at the same place?"

"Hey my friend and I were having a debate about the best restaurant in the area, do you have a favorite?" If they say no, ask if they have lived in the area for a while or if they just moved.

Questions or comments about the environment. Things like "this convention centre is huge, isn't it?" or "Bob's house is really beautiful isn't it? I've never been here before."

So on and so forth. The key here is to know that the conversation starters you choose just need to be simple and applicable to almost any situation. They are open ended but specific enough so they do not to put the other person on the spot.

Keeping the conversation flowing

The best way to keep a conversation flowing is to ask questions about what the person just said but sometimes that topic just dies down and there's no saving it. This is when you can now use a conversation topic that is often listed as a "conversation starter" but is really a way to prolong an already started conversation. Again these topics work best if they are tailored to your interests. Here are some examples:

-Seen any good movies lately?

-So, got any plans for the weekend?

-Any vacations planned in the near future?

-Did you hear about [insert latest news topic]?

The good thing about those topics is if their answer is "no", they're probably going to ask you if you have seen a good movie, have weekend plans etc. This is why you have to have your answer to these already planned in your head so that you can go on talking about them and answer the question if they didn't have an answer. This is a way to fool proof those conversation topics because you know you can talk about them. Never ask a question that you don't have an answer to yourself.

There's nothing wrong with having a "go-to" story

I worked in the film industry for many years and the company I worked for was always looking to source new clients. My boss could win the gold medal in the small talk Olympics and one of his techniques was to have a go-to story. I often watched him repeat the same stories to many potential clients and he'd even repeat full conversations with the same perfectly timed jokes. He'd often tell these stories over and over again, but always to people he had just met. So even though the stories were boring for me, the person he was talking to was always very impressed.

My boss taught me that it's a good thing to have a story that you always pull out of your pocket, even if your close friends have heard it before. If the person you are talking to hasn't heard it, pull it out and get the conversation rolling.

Dish out some compliments

A word of caution is that you should keep it subtle. Don't go overboard and shower them with praise. Just avoid coming across as awkward or cheesy. If you notice someone being nice to the waiters, start your conversation with something like, "It's rare to find someone who treats waiters with such kindness, btw my name is___. How's your day going?" See what I did there? After complimenting someone, don't get stuck. Quickly move away from the praise and follow it up with a casual question about the weather, the place or how their day has been turning out.

Some people may not be used to being appreciated, and it may startle them to know that a stranger is throwing them a compliment. But when you immediately direct the conversation toward something else, they feel comfortable. That way it doesn't get too awkward, and it allows a moment for the other person to process the compliment.

Appreciating someone is a sweet way of communicating with someone.

Compliments are also way easier to slip into a conversation that is already happening rather than using it is a starter. Saying something like "that's hilarious, you are so funny!" "yeah that's true, you sound really smart" sounds a lot more genuine if it's said in passing.

So now we've covered the general mindset that you need to adopt to master small talk. In the next few chapters I'm going to highlight the most common situations where you might need to use these skills and specific techniques you will need to succeed in those situations.

Chapter Five: Small Talk for People with Social Anxiety

Your social anxiety is a real thing. It may be irrational, it may not make sense, it may be "stupid" but it's really there. I have a fear of spiders. Even small tiny ones will have me screaming and running in the opposite direction. I'm really lucky to have a boyfriend that can kill these spiders for me so I never have to deal with them – or am I? As much as I cringe to admit this, him being there to kill those spiders is ensuring that I remain scared of spiders for the rest of my life.

Now when I say I'm afraid of spiders, it's not just little ones that you see in your bathtub. I can't even look at a photo of a tarantula or any spider on the internet (or worse, on video) without feeling shivers race through my body which causes an immediate scream and covering of my eyes. I feel my heartbeat increase, I feel my hands start to sweat and the sense of panic is very overwhelming.

So let's imagine that I want to overcome this fear. The worst thing that I could do and the one thing that is guaranteed to make my fear solidified in me for life, is taking on the grand prize right away. In this case, that would be something like holding a tarantula. I can't even look at a photo of one on Google, never mind looking at one or touching one in real life! If anyone put me in this situation, I would have a panic attack and never attempt to overcome my fear ever again. It would be a very traumatic experience.

This is the same principle that you are facing with your social anxiety. If you have a fear of social situations, no person saying "just put yourself out there" or "come on it will be fun" is going to help that. If you listen to those people, you might find yourself holding a tarantula. This could be a party where you don't know anyone or other social event where you feel completely lost and out of your comfort zone. You need to start small and prepare yourself appropriately. If I'm about to look at a spider in real life, I better know it's happening so I can prepare – surprises are not fun when they are your worst fear.

Being by yourself in a room is not scary

There's nothing wrong with preparing for a social situation. Remember that small talk is about mindset, it's not about conversation topics. This means you have to get yourself in the right frame of mind where it's the easiest to do this – by yourself, in your home. Getting yourself in the right frame of mind when you're in the middle of a big party is a recipe for disaster.

Now, this doesn't mean you spend hours pondering over what you will talk about and how you wish to come across to other people. Of course, you will have a few conversation starters memorized, but that's not the only aspect of preparation. It means trying to think positively about the situation, going for a walk to reduce your anxiety about attending the event, taking a warm bubble bath or listening to some soothing music that will calm your nerves down. Self care is at the root of everything we do. You need to ensure that the time before attending the event should be spent in calming yourself rather than fretting over how you are going to handle the situation. When you get into a lighter and more upbeat mood, you will automatically be attuned to your feelings and will have great conversations as a result. This will also induce more positive feelings about the people you are going to encounter at the event.

Take baby steps

The first step in overcoming the fear is to start at a level that is reasonable. Ideally you would find a social situation that makes you slightly uncomfortable but not too much. If this is not possible and you find yourself at a big party, just remember you don't need to make everyone pay attention to you or be the life of the party in order to participate. All you need to do at this point is to engage with a small group. Start with one-on-one conversations, and then slowly move on to smaller groups. Avoid interacting with a larger group for now as you are just starting to feel comfortable and should avoid anything that makes you nervous.

If all you do all night is talk to a few people, that's amazing. Be sure to celebrate the small wins. If you feel up to it, join a small group and use your body language techniques to engage in the conversation. This means laughing, nodding and showing signs that you're listening, you don't even need to say anything and people will see you as part of the group. Always remember that this was a huge step you took to get out of your comfort zone, so give yourself some credit.

Remember that small talk is simple

The best part about small talk is that you really don't have to try too hard. Everyone that is in a conversation with someone they just met knows this isn't going to a deep and meaningful place. All humans understand that small talk is simple and boring. Use this fact to take some of the pressure off. If you are making generic comments about the room you're in or the drinks your drinking don't let the negative Nancy in your head tell you that you are being boring. Everyone is boring at the beginning. Just take a step back and enjoy the moment.

Opening your conversation with small talk also helps you measure up the other person's interest in the conversation. If you get an emphatic response, then you can carry on your conversation, but if you receive a vague answer in a luke-warm tone, you can use one of the escape routes we talked about earlier to remove yourself from the situation. Remember there's always an out, you've memorized and practiced how to get out of a conversation so if things are not going well, you can always save yourself.

Try to keep the conversations light. Don't start by talking about what you think about the government, space, history or the meaning of life. Not everyone is willing to talk about topics that need more mental energy. Remember, this is just an opening act. You can always steer the conversation in another direction at a later stage.

Try to speak about what you fear

When I was in college, I had a friend who was socially very awkward. So when I insisted on her attending the annual college party, she was initially very reluctant, but eventually agreed to join us. She turned up looking very stunning in a long, flowy gown. Naturally, everyone wanted to strike up a conversation with her, but she got so nervous that she literally curled up into a corner. A friend noticed her discomfort and he went up to her to ask if everything was okay. She confessed to him that she was feeling extremely anxious, and didn't know what to talk about. That was enough to take their conversation further, and they ended up having a blast at the party. They are still good friends and very much in touch with each other.

When you talk about your fears, you evoke a feeling of empathy from the other person. It makes them want to connect with you without feeling any discomfort. What often stops us from openly saying things like, "I am feeling a little nervous right now," or "I get uncomfortable when faced with crowds," is our deep fear of making ourselves look weak in front of people. Revealing our discomfort with certain things makes us vulnerable, but vulnerability attracts deeper relationships.

Get out of your head

Remember that your thoughts in a small talk conversation are going to be your own worst enemy if you have social anxiety. Your thoughts will filter out good comments so that you never say them and your thoughts will dwell on bad or awkward comments that you did say out loud. A great way to stop the inner voice is to practice talking to yourself alone at home. I know it sounds weird, but trust me it works. People with social anxiety, and introverts like me often think a lot. They love to be in their head and their head is constantly analyzing and over thinking. The best way to kill this talking banshee in our heads is to talk out loud. It's a lot more difficult to think when you're talking so practice talking at home in front of the mirror for 2 or 3 minutes at a time to get used to the feeling of talking without thinking. Practicing this for a few weeks will do wonders for your small talking skills.

Chapter Six: Small Talk for introverts

A lot of the tips that I gave on small talk for social anxiety can apply to people who are introverts but it's not 100% the same. If you are an introvert, this means that you don't have an irrational fear that you are trying to overcome. It simply means that you would prefer to be at home watching your favorite show or hanging out with your friends rather than be at a huge party.

Don't let the fact that you are introverted allow yourself to justify why you can't get better at something. Imagine the most extroverted person you know. Wouldn't it be nice if he or she was better at listening and remembering stories that they've already told? The answer is yes!

Your Introversion is not an anxiety

The best part about being introverted and not having social anxiety is that you're not afraid of social situations, you just find them draining. It's like me when I was in University. It wasn't that I was afraid or insecure about myself, I just wanted to be in the library reading a book.

This is an advantage for you because all you need to do is perfect the small talk skills we discussed, and then you'll find yourself actually enjoying that party. If you find a small group of people who are chatting about things you like, you're actually going to have a lot of fun.

So think about learning how to small talk like a small hurdle that will eventually lead to something more enjoyable. It's like when you learn to play the guitar. At first you're bad at it and it hurts your fingers, but once you get over that part you're going to have a lot of fun.

Don't put too much pressure on yourself

There are plenty of extroverts at the party that are going to love being the center of attention. The great news is you can enjoy the show safely from a distance. Marching right ahead toward people you find interesting, and immediately starting small talk isn't always necessary. You can be grounded in your own energy by being easy about everything and people will start flocking around you without you doing much. If you don't feel like disclosing too much information about yourself during a conversation, simply don't.

Remember to elaborate on your responses

If someone asks how your day has been, don't just stop at, "It was good." Further your response with something like, "It was good, but I wish I could have gotten home earlier from work, you know to relax myself. Sometimes you need that me time don't you?" That way, the other person can either ask you further questions or add to the existing topic at hand. This trick helps you to avoid the conversation remaining stagnant and much substance can be added as it progresses.

As an introvert this is going to be the one area where statistically it's going to be harder for you. You can talk about yourself, it's ok. Don't automatically assume that you are boring people, in fact most people are interested in listening to others and hearing their story.

Do not brood over goof-ups

I mentioned this a bit in the last chapter but wanted to re-iterate this because I struggle with this a lot and I'm introverted. Remember, what's done is done, there is no use dwelling on the past. Put your overthinking into perspective by asking these questions:

- Am I simply overanalyzing what happened?
- Am I too hard on myself?
- Is this self-analysis lifting my spirits or bringing me down?

Stop when you think you might be analyzing yourself too much. You know the best part about self-reflection is that you have the power to change yourself, but see to it that it doesn't make you change your inherent nature.

Take time to recuperate

Meeting social and professional obligations isn't easy for us introverts, and therefore we need to take time off occasionally to recuperate. Most introverts feel drained after having too many conversations with too many people, especially if it involves small talk so there's nothing wrong with re-charging for a few minutes by going to get a drink or stepping outside.

The big thing that I need to stress here is not to take too long of a break. If you are in a social situation and you go off outside, you're going to be right where you want to be: alone and in your head so that you can think. This is going to feel nice and you're going to want to stay there. Looking inwards at the crowd of people is going to feel way more daunting and you're just going to want to leave. So keep the breaks really short and plan your real re-charge time for when you get home.

The difference between talking to an extrovert vs. an introvert

A useful thing to remember is that the dynamic of the conversation will change slightly depending on if you're taking to an extrovert or introvert. There are pros and cons to both and you might find you prefer one over the other.

Extrovert

When you're talking to extrovert, it's going to be a lot easier to listen and to encourage them to keep talking. This can take a lot of the pressure off because you just need to ask them a simple question and they will likely go on about it for a while. Extroverts are also really natural at filling the silence so you can relax knowing that they will probably fill in any pauses.

All of this sounds great as an introvert but one downside is that your energy level is likely a lot lower than the extrovert's. This means they might get bored of the conversation quickly and may want to move on to talking to someone else. A way to avoid this is to remember the first key to small talk which is *enthusiasm*. If you make an effort to make an exaggerated reaction to what they're saying, they will enjoy the attention and want to keep talking.

Introvert

The great thing about talking to another introvert is that they'll totally understand where you're coming from. They probably also don't like small talk and so it's likely that they'll want to take the conversation to something deeper more quickly than an extrovert would. This can be great for you because then you can really start having a fun and meaningful conversation. The likelihood of making a good friend out this kind of situation is also really high since you are both connecting so well on a deeper level.

The downside of talking to a fellow introvert that you don't know is the conversation could get stuck really easily. If you are not finding a deeper conversation that you both enjoy, you'll find yourself stuck in awkward small talk that never moves forward. Knowing this, your conversation topics and questions are going to be a lot more useful than the listening and body language skills. You'll need to be more comfortable with doing the talking and filling in any gaps.

Now that you have an idea of how the conversation will go with both extroverts and introverts, you know which techniques to pull out of your pocket at which time.

Consider giving up on the end game

One of the biggest shifts in your approach toward small talk will be to completely give up on your expectations of any outcome. It wasn't until I stopped this compelling need to meet everyone's expectations so they could be my friends that I started making more connections. Life isn't always going to turn out the way you want. Sometimes you may feel that small talk is getting you nowhere and you start questioning whether there is any point in trying to talk to people anymore. The problem isn't small talk, but it's your laser focus on the outcome that needs to be diverted elsewhere. Rather than having an agenda in mind, when you approach people out of pure curiosity, you will not only make new friends but also actually enjoy the process. When you are not "outcome focused," you will end up getting what you want.

Chapter Seven: Small Talk for Dates

Do you get nervous when you're getting ready for a big date? If you are not fan of small talk, you will find it even more frustrating when you go on dates. Dates are all about small talk. It's basically agreeing to small talk with someone you don't know for a whole hour or more, what a nightmare!

Did you start agreeing with me in that paragraph above? If so, it was a test and you failed! Remember, small talk is about *mindset*. If you go into it thinking this is going to be a nightmare, you're already setting yourself up to fail. You already know the two keys to small talk are *enthusiasm* and *intrigue* and you are going to use those skills to nail those dates. That being said, a date can be a little different than some other social events so here are some tips you need to know for small talking on a date.

It's okay that you are nervous, but don't bring it up

A lot of people get nervous on dates, it's perfectly normal. If you look a bit nervous or are stumbling on your words, the person will completely understand – dates are awkward for everybody. The one thing that I would avoid though is mentioning that you're nervous. That just calls attention to it and gets them looking at signs of nervousness instead of listening to you. No good. If you look nervous, they will forgive you but if you call it out, things will get awkward.

Dates allow you to get more personal

Most of the time dates flow into more serious conversation pretty easily because both parties are looking to get to know each other. This makes it more socially acceptable to ask personal questions like "so what's your family like?" when you wouldn't really ask that at a networking event.

Dates are this weird social situation where you actually can get out of the small talk mode and into the serious talk mode pretty quickly. Since you guys are both in a place where you're looking to see if the other person is going to be a long-term fit, you can get away with personal questions and stories about your childhood. I would stay away from *super* personal questions like wanting kids, wanting to get married or talking about an ex but those are pretty much the only taboo topics on a date.

Pick a conversation friendly date location

If you happen to be the one picking the place, you can pick one that can gives you something to talk about; places like a coffee house inside a historical place or a pizza corner with a lot of interesting history attached to it. Interesting places like this make it easy to comment on if the conversation starts to die down. A place that has a pool table or other kind of distraction can also break up the monotony of sitting across from each other.

Talk about what you like to do in your free time

Talking about your hobbies is a great way to get the conversation ball rolling. It might seem cliché, but that's ok on a date – dates are cliché and formulaic. Everyone knows this going into it so they're not going to judge you for it. Just remember not to go on and on about what you like. Talk about some fun things you like to do and see if they're showing interest. If they are, go ahead and elaborate. Show them pictures of the recent trek you went on or places you traveled. Say something about why you took on a particular hobby. For instance, you took to extreme sports because you wanted to make your life more exciting, or that you started photography because you realized your passion for nature and how capturing it with your camera gives you immense joy. That being said, never hold the spotlight for too long, always turn the conversation back to them after a few minutes.

Don't showcase low self esteem in your talks

Don't get me wrong. You can certainly talk about weaknesses at some point in time during the conversation and that may make you appear more honest. But don't go on a self-depreciating binge by saying something like, "I have always felt inferior to others," "I am not that smart," or "I think other girls are prettier than me." Who likes to hear such negative statements on their dates? Even if you believe such claims, don't mention them in front of your date. Not only will you start getting convinced about the things you talk about but your date may also start thinking the same thing.

Sometimes we end up saying bad things about ourselves because we are secretly fishing for compliments. We expect the other person to come up with something like, "Who says you are not that smart? You seem pretty smart to me." Trust me; it's a recipe for disaster. It can create a very negative picture of you in the mind of your date. The bottom line is make no self-depreciating comments that will leave your date overwhelmed.

Awesome date questions

As always, questions are the best way to use the second key to small talk which is *intrigue.* As I said before, there aren't many taboo topics on a date but you don't want to overwhelm the person with a bunch of questions. This isn't an interrogation. You should be focused on building a rapport and getting to know the other person. Here are a few questions you can ask your date:

- What do you do on weekends?
- How was it growing up in _____ (city)?
- What do you do for a living?
- Do you have a bucket list?
- Is there a movie that fascinates you?

Talk about pet peeves

People love talking about what annoys them the most. Also knowing about someone's pet peeves helps you to know what to avoid in future so this is an excellent date topic that is sure to get the ball rolling.

This is a topic of conversation that I don't think you have to sneak in there. You can just straight up ask "so, what are some of your pet peeves" and you'll likely get a good response. Remember that when you ask questions like this, you should always have your own answer ready in case they say "I don't have any, what are yours?"

Chapter Eight: Small Talk for Making Friends

Small talk isn't some fad that people have recently started using. It's been used as a mode of communication for thousands of years. So, it's obvious that there must be a good reason for it. When it comes to making new friends, you will need something in common to talk about. As you break into a conversation, and you use small talk to briefly touch on a wide variety of topics, you will find out if you have something in common with the other person. You can, by all means, talk about the deeper stuff but save it for later or let it get to that point organically.

Have High Hopes

Remember, small talk is *mindset*. This step is always number one. Even if you possess great skills to help you make friends, your thoughts could make you feel negative about yourself, and you will end up nowhere. If you assume that small talk is pointless or dull, it is going to be exactly that. This is especially important to remember when making friends. Why?

Because you're never going to be at a "making friends" event. You can be at job interviews, networking events or a date but making a friend can happen anywhere. This is why having high hopes when you talk to *anyone* is the first way to start making your small talk work for you.

Just think: this person that just commented about the weather could be your new best friend. The one who buys you shots on your birthday when you don't want them. The one that helps you move on a Tuesday. Responding with a "yeah, sure is nice out these days" doesn't seem so bad when you look at it like that.

Spot someone who is ready for a chat

The best way to start making friends with small talk is to look for a person who is open for a conversation and is easy to talk to. You don't want to get turned down by people, which can discourage you from approaching others. As soon as you walk into a bar or a party, look around and notice who is ready for a chat. This is something you will have to figure out from their body language, facial expressions or by noticing how interested, they seem in their surroundings.

You can't chat up people who are waiting to ride in the elevator peacefully. But at the same time, if you spot someone who has a chirpy disposition, an open body language or a smiling face, you can approach them without any hesitation. On the other hand, if you find them consistently looking in the opposite direction, then they are probably interested in having a moment of Zen or not in the mood of idle banter. Once you pick a person who shows an equal amount of interest, the conversation will flow smoothly.

Chapter Nine: Small Talk for Networking and Business events

As always, we have to start with mindset so let's think about it logically. A networking event is set up so that you can meet people. It's not a place to chit chat with the people you already know. When you remember this, you remember that everyone else at the event is there to meet people. This makes it way easier to butt into a conversation or to introduce yourself because people are expecting this to happen. It's the entire reason why everyone is there.

One way to thrive while you meet new people for networking is to be a good storyteller. You can come up with stories that perfectly combine your personal and professional life. When you tell a story, it has to make a clear point along with having a strong punch line. If you look around, most people come across as boring or hesitant in the way they communicate. You can change this using some simple techniques. Have a look below:

Look Approachable and act classy

Don't get stuck sitting in a corner sipping on a drink. I know this from firsthand experience, the longer you actively try to avoid socializing, the harder it gets. If you start the day guns a blazing going around and introducing yourself, it can be a great way to get the ball rolling in your own mind. It's a way to tell yourself "you got this." If you sit in a corner or start looking at your phone, you're going to get stuck there.

The best way to come across as approachable is to have a pleasant smile on your face, especially when someone looks your way. Studies say that putting a smile on our faces makes you look super approachable and attractive. Some reports also suggest that people are 86% more likely to have a conversation with strangers when they are smiling. Use this to your advantage throughout the evening.

Perfect the humble confident balance

Having confidence is a good thing, but you don't want to come across as overbearing. You should try your best to come across as both humble and confident at the same time. Here is a list of traits that fall into each category. Try to pick a few from each one so that you maintain balance.

Confident:

- Loud voice

- Talks a lot

- Uses big hand gestures

- Is very knowledgeable about the topics he/she speaks about

- Doesn't show signs of nervousness, like playing with his/her hands or twirling a straw

- Quick to fill awkward silences

- Has exaggerated facial expressions to keep people's attention

- Laughs loudly

- Isn't afraid of being the center of attention

- Enjoys talking about him or herself

- Maintains eye contact

Humble:

- Listens to people and their stories

- Asks follow up questions so that the other person keeps talking

- Soft voice and minimal hand gestures

- Is warm and comforting, makes other people feel comfortable

- Doesn't put other people on the spot

- Deflects the spotlight onto others

Use the person's name

Never forget the name of the person you are talking to during the conversation. As Dale Carnegie said, the sweetest sound to one's ears is the sound of their own name. People won't necessarily tell you this, but they appreciate it when you mention their name. Be sure to thank the person by using their first name when you are leaving.

Arrive early

It's not a casual party, so arriving late isn't going to raise your stakes. In fact, you may lose out on important contacts you can establish at the start of the event. When you arrive a few minutes earlier than the event time, you get enough time to get a feel for the event and are able to find time for easy small talk. You can start introducing yourself to people as they keep arriving, and you can also fall back on the same set of people as the event starts getting crowded.

Bring a friend along

Some experts are of the opinion that bringing along a colleague or a friend can hinder your ability to make conversation with new people, while some say it can actually be helpful. Personally, it has always helped me make a positive impression whenever I bring a friend along. It's a common weapon to kill the awkwardness that comes with such events. I always bring my friend along to networking events and introduce him as someone I work with. It helps us look like a team, makes it easier to have a conversation with a larger group of people, and keeps me accountable as he keeps reminding me about my goals, and I end up focusing more. I suggest trying this both ways to see what works best for you.

Conclusion

Don't you love knowing that mastering the art of small talk doesn't involve coming up with things to say? The fact that you picked up this book and read it from front to back means you're serious about improving your skills. Just doing that shows me that you know that learning and mindset are the keys to getting what you want and I hope this book was able to help you out. Remember practice makes perfect.

I wanted to present my readers with practical ways of handling different situations with the help of small talk. The conversation guidelines in this book will help you feel comfortable even in the most seemingly uncomfortable situations. There's almost always room for enhancing your conversational skills.

Becoming a good conversationalist is going to improve the quality of your life, and it's going to have an amazing ripple effect. It will bring in new people, new opportunities and you will be beaming with confidence before you know it.

One final thing I'll say is that it's good to learn from other people. As you know from my book, I was an introvert deathly afraid of small talk and I learned how to do it by watching others who were better at it than I was. People like that friendly school teacher and my boss were great examples. Never underestimate learning by just watching what other people do. Now that you've read this book, it will be easier to spot people who are using these skills well. Watch what they do and try to imitate them in your own way.

Free Bonus: 100 Fool Proof Conversation Starters

Since my whole book was based on the mindset of small talk, I refrained from listing off a bunch of conversation starters. I did this because I think it's important to attack the root of the problem rather than just covering it up by memorizing one liners.

Now that you know how to build a solid foundation, I'd like to offer you my list of 100 Fool-Proof Conversation Starters as a bonus for reading my book. If you're interested in getting it, please visit: https://millennialships.lpages.co/conversation-starters/

Thanks for picking up my book on small talk, I wish you the best of luck!

Made in the USA
San Bernardino, CA
21 July 2019